C000271526

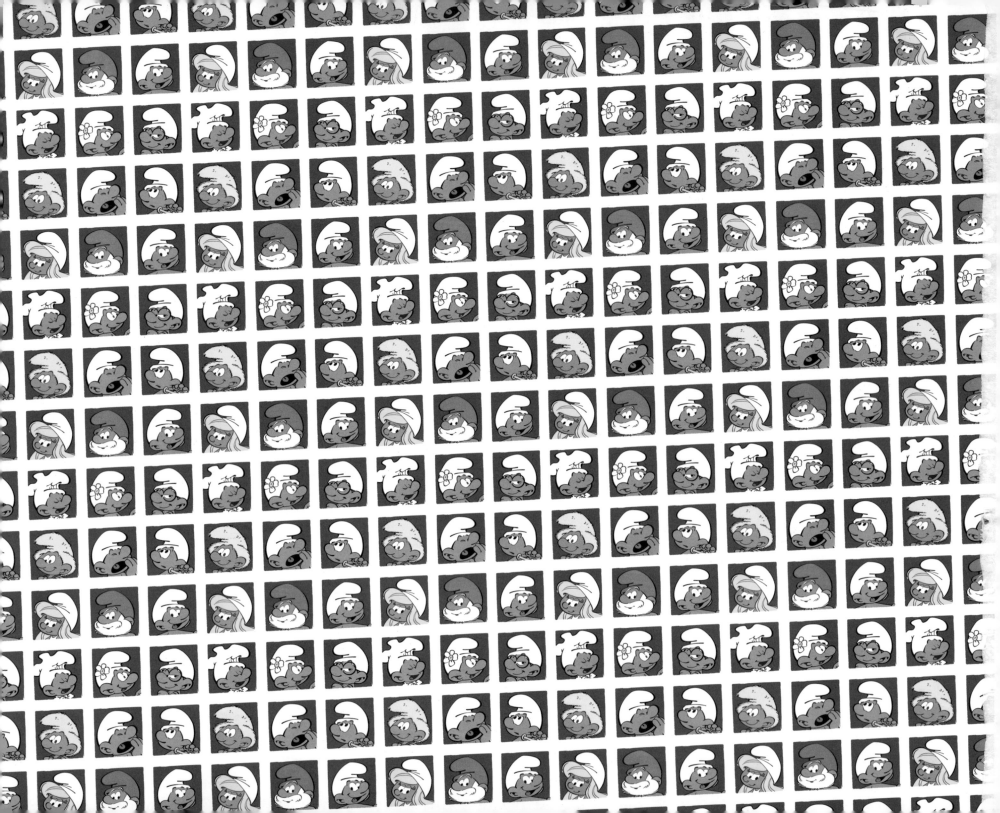

The World of
SMURFS

A CELEBRATION OF TINY BLUE PROPORTIONS

by Matt. Murray

academic school, but found the other students more advanced than he, and, again, dropped out.

At fifteen, Pierre was forced to enter the adult world and find a job. A film lover, he took a job as an assistant projectionist at a local movie house. While he hated the German propaganda of the newsreels he ran, he relished the opportunity to watch free movies. Ultimately, he found the actual work (the spooling and rewinding of reels in a cramped closet for hours on end) tedious, and, as it was a solitary job, he sought camaraderie in the friends he had made as a scout.

After two years, Pierre was feeling fed up with the low-paying life of a projectionist. For side work, he performed numerous odd jobs—like decorating lampshades, which did engage his artistic abilities—but he was completely unsatisfied with life as he knew it. One day, he decided to comb the classifieds. Two ads caught his eye—one was for a dental assistant, the other was to apprentice at a small animation studio formed by la Compagnie Belge d'Actualités.

He went to the dentist's office to find that the position had been filled just minutes before his arrival, leaving the C.B.A. as his only hope of getting out of the projection booth.

OPPOSITE | Pierre (on the right) working as a cel painter at the C.B.A. **RIGHT |** Young Pierre on the streets of Brussels c. 1946.

"J'arriverai!"

In 1945 the C.B.A. hired seventeen-year-old Pierre Culliford for its ink-and-paint department—much to the young artist's surprise—but the work wouldn't last long. Within months of his hiring, the C.B.A. shut down and Pierre lost his job. While some animators would find work at the Belgian comics anthology, *Le Journal Spirou*, the editors found Pierre's work to be weaker than the others and didn't hire him.

In order to build his drafting skills, he began studying at the Académie Royale des Beaux-Arts, but after three months he found himself more interested in socializing than sitting through drawing classes. During this time, he would meet one girl in particular who would capture his heart, Janine "Nine" Devroye. The two would date for close to five years before finally getting married on June 9, 1951.

During those five years, Pierre completely dedicated himself to getting a job as an artist. Most of his work came in advertising: drawing ads for local shops or logos for paper shopping bags. All the while, he never gave up his aspirations to become a cartoonist with his own comic strip in the Sunday comic supplements

LEFT | In November 1946, Pierre met Janine Devroye through a mutual friend. The two dated for nearly five years before getting married.

of newspapers or in the pages of magazines like *Spirou,* or *Le Journal Tintin,* which began publishing after the war.

In 1946 Pierre managed to sell a few short stories about the Indian warrior Pied-Tendre (Tenderfoot) and his scout Puce (Chip) to the comics section of *L'Occident.* That same year, *Bon Marché* bought a Tintin-inspired comic called "Une aventure de l'inspecteur Pik" for its *Le Petit Monde* supplement; and *La Dernière Heure* would pick up the first installments of *Johan,* an adventure strip about a medieval page boy. By this point he had begun to sign his work "Peyo," and while he hadn't necessarily made a proper name for himself, his now-famous signature had begun to take shape.

Although he failed to sell other adventure strips, like the pirate saga *Capitaine Coky,* Culliford still managed to find steady advertising work while trying to develop more comics. In 1949, he noticed a trend toward funny animals and created *Poussy,* a gag strip about a cat, which was purchased by *Le Soir.* A success, *Poussy* led to the newspaper picking up further adventures of Johan from the artist, and both comics would enjoy long runs in that paper.

RIGHT | Rare color work done by Peyo in the late 1940s. (CLOCKWISE FROM LEFT) A 1949 cover for the magazine *Le Moustique,* his first work for Dupuis; an early panel illustration of *Poussy* (also 1949); and a 1947 cartoon depicting a camping trip taken with Nine, who is shown at the head of the pack.

" . . . [Franquin] responded, `Look, here's the schtroumpf, and when you've finished schtroumpfing, schtroumpf it back to me!' It was so fun to schtroumpf for the few days we spent together, it became a joke for us."

—Peyo

vain to learn to speak "Schtroumpf," allowing for some comical moments to break up the action, and ultimately the Schtroumpfs and the humans are able to work together to beat the villain and restore life to normal.

Like Pirlouit before them, the Schtroumpfs were a huge success delivered in a small package. Popular demand had them appearing in the next *Johan et Pirlouit* adventure, "La Guerre des sept fontaines" (1959), and that same year the little blue gnomes were tapped to help kick off a new publishing initiative from *Spirou*, "mini-récits."

A self-folding supplement to be removed from the pages of *Spirou*, mini-récits (little stories) gave readers a

LEFT | (TOP) Peyo c. the mid-1950s, just prior to the vacation that would birth the word "Schtroumpf." (BOTTOM) Panels taken from the 1959 mini-récit "Le Voleur de Schtroumpfs" ("The Smurfnapper").

fully contained forty-eight-page story in a postcard-sized comic. Yvan Delporte, who had recently been installed as Editor-in-Chief, recognized that the diminutive stature of the Schtroumpfs made them the perfect stars for these mini-comics. Dupuis approached Peyo about the idea, and he agreed, on the condition that Delporte help him write the comic.

Their first effort, "Les Schtroumpfs noirs," had the Schtroumpfs battling themselves as the village fell victim to a disease caused by a sting from a "Bzz" fly. A basic allegory for the Black Plague that spread through Europe during the Middle Ages, "Les Schtroumpfs noirs" helped establish the basic setting and some of the original characters that would become the staples of the series, and introduced Delporte's role as a collaborator in the creative process. While Peyo had ultimate control of the storylines and characters, Delporte would help develop the particulars of the plot and write the dialogue before Peyo committed the final script to paper and created the artwork. Though they had two very different personal styles and occasionally had clashing ideas, the collaboration served to strengthen the storytelling and would last for the rest of Peyo's professional career.

RIGHT | Selected pages from the mini-récit "Les Schtroumpfs noirs" (1959).

Unfortunately, early attempts at building the marionettes showed that the characters' oversized heads made the puppets too top-heavy and difficult to maneuver properly, so the project never fully materialized.

Recognizing Peyo's rising stardom, Dupuis insisted that Peyo make *Poussy* a full-page strip strictly for the readers of *Spirou*. The artist acquiesced, although he didn't want to completely sever his ties with *Le Soir*, the paper that gave him his early taste of success. In an effort to create a new comic for *Le Soir*, he devised *Benoît Brisefer* (later imported to English-speaking countries as *Stephen Strong*), a strip about a little boy with Herculean strength, but Dupuis liked that idea as well and purchased the comics for *Spirou*.

Peyo finally ended up selling *Jacky et Célestin* (about the adventures of two kids in Brussels) to *Le Soir*, but with five regular comics to attend to, he found himself spread thin and began to amass a team of assistants to help him with his output. He stayed firmly involved with the creation and development of each property, often establishing the plot and then laying out the

LEFT | (Clockwise from top) A still from a TVA Dupuis Schtroumpf television short; a character illustration of Poussy taken from a Spirou promotional poster; Benoît Brisefer bounds across the cover of a 1961 Spirou collection. **OPPOSITE |** Peyo c. 1964. **PREVIOUS |** The artist at his desk, kept company by a little blue buddy.

panels of any given comic before handing the work off to an assistant to fill in the details of an illustration and work with Nine on coloring before sending it out for editorial approval.

Soon Peyo found himself the head of a studio, leading a team of artists much in the way Jijé had done with the Gang of Four and the Marcinelle School. His old friend Will was handed the artistic reigns on *Jacky* and a rotating team of assistants—which at various points included Francis, Derib, Walthery, Wasterlain, and Gos (who all achieved solo success later in their careers)—handled his other strips including *Poussy*, *Benoît Brisefer*, and *Les Schtroumpfs*. Other associates, such as Franquin, would lend an occasional hand, and, after leaving his official post at *Spirou*, Delporte would continue to provide written material for Peyo.

However, with the development of modern marketing and the breakout success of his characters, Pierre Culliford's role as the head of "Studio Peyo" wasn't just an artistic title but one of increasing responsibility in the selling of his creations, especially *Les Schtroumpfs*.

OPPOSITE | Peyo, c. 1964, laying the groundwork for the future careers of his children: Thierry (at left, born in 1956), who would grow up to write and illustrate the *Smurfs* comics; and Véronique (at right, born in 1958), who would eventually manage the business and marketing ends of her father's empire as the President of I.M.P.S. **LEFT |** The artist ca. 1964 (TOP) and 1967 (BOTTOM).

GLOBAL VILLAGE

WHILE "LES SCHTROUMPFS" were a national treasure in Belgium, it would take the contributions of a Dutch singer, a British petroleum company, an American television executive, and thousands of international companies to make the Smurfs a worldwide phenomenon.

By the end of the 1980s, millions of children would be calling them various names, from *"Los Pitufos"* (in Spanish); to *"Hupikék Törpikék"* (in Hungarian); to *"Die Schlümpfe"* (in German); to *"Il Puffi"* (in Italian); but it would be the Dutch translation, *"De Smurfen,"* that would help identify them for English speakers.

The Smurfs would take the world by storm.

Song of the Smurfs

In 1977, to promote the European release of the film *La Flûte à Six Schtroumpfs*, Dupuis, through its licensing arm—La Société d'Edition, de Presse et de Publicité (S.E.P.P.)—reached out to children's entertainer Vader Abraham (Father Abraham, to English speakers) to record a song for the Dutch market.

"The Smurf Song" became an instant hit, quickly selling out of its initial pressing, and a full-length album was commissioned. The record was translated into numerous languages and sold throughout Europe where it went gold, selling over five-hundred thousand copies. It spawned chart-topping singles in sixteen countries. The English translation of "The Smurf Song"

was the United Kingdom's sixth best-selling record of 1978, preparing that country for one of the most popular marketing campaigns in Smurf history.

That same year, S.E.P.P. contracted with National Benzole (later known as British Petroleum) to launch the "Service with a Smurf!" program, which gave buyers a free Smurf PVC figurine with the purchase of gasoline at participating National service stations. According to BBC News, the "promotion quickly turned the two-inch-high pixies into the hottest currency in school playgrounds," securing the Smurfs a strong foothold in the English-speaking market.

S.E.P.P. was determined to use the popularity of the British campaign to cross over into the American marketplace; however, they had difficulties in finding a company that would support foreign characters depicted in plastic. Most distributors wanted to place their own label on recognizable stuffed dolls.

In 1979, Wallace Berrie & Co. acquired the North American licensing rights to the Smurfs and began to import their own versions of the PVC figures using preexisting molds from Dupuis, Bully, and Schleich. While most PVC toys sold for roughly twenty-five cents

LEFT | French singer Dorothée is one of many international artists who have found success through a musical association with Les Schtroumpfs. **PREVIOUS |** Peyo and Nine Culliford c. 1982. "She was his muse *and* his partner," recalls their daughter Véronique. "She had final say as to whether something was 'good' or not."

LaLaLaLaLaLaLa

in the late 1970s, Wallace Berrie took the risk of plac-
ing the Smurfs in American stores at the price of
$1.50, which, to the surprise of the toy
industry, didn't deter shop-
pers from snapping
up the little guys
(and girl). The com-
pany reinvested the
revenue into creating
more products, includ-
ing Smurfs plush dolls,
which became highly
sought-after cuddly collectibles in the United States.

As the toys grew in popu-
larity, the comics were translated and brought over to the
United States, but full-blown
Smurf-mania had yet to grab the
country or the world. It would take
a well-placed stuffed Smurf to truly
launch that craze . . .

RIGHT | An international superstar thanks to the success of the
"The Smurf Song" and the toys, Peyo signs autographs for Spanish
fans (CENTER), and takes a spin with one of his blue buddies c.
late 1970s (RIGHT).

Saturday Morning Superstars

The "Golden Age of Saturday Morning Cartoons" was a period from 1966 to 1990 when all three American television networks (yes, there were only three: ABC, CBS, and NBC) made a conscious decision to devote blocks of their weekend morning programming exclusively to animated programming intended for children. Early stars of this period were superheroes like Birdman and fictional teenaged rock bands like The Archies, but as time went on, live-action kids' shows and other family-friendly programming began to take over the airwaves, the ratings started to dip, and the future of Saturday morning cartoons as an institution began to seem uncertain.

The late 1970s were an especially bleak time for animated cartoons. Network programmers and animation studios had fallen into a pattern of reusing popular formulas—assembling groups of teenaged crime solvers around a unique mascot character in the *Scooby-Doo* vein, for example. Some just took characters from their most popular shows and paired them together, making them "perform" or "compete" much like their live-action

LEFT | From left to right: A Smurf matching card game from 1975, and a checklist of available Smurf products offered in the U.S. by Wallace-Berrie, so consumers could keep track of their collections. **OPPOSITE |** Peyo in his studio c. 1982.

Cameron, then a story editor (and the first woman to hold that title in Hanna-Barbera's history), stated that: "One of the symbols we will demonstrate in this episode includes the sign of the cat, so the Smurfs can warn each other about Azrael without the cat hearing them. Another important one is the symbol for 'I Love You,' which is the thought expressed in every *Smurfs* episode we write."

Her contributions as writer helped the show to win its second Daytime Emmy for Outstanding Children's Entertainment Series in 1984 (its prior win in that category was in the previous year) and *The Smurfs* would be nominated for a total of five more Emmys in the category of Outstanding Animated Series. In 1987, the show and writers Burnett and John Loy would also win a Humanitas Prize for "writers whose work explores the human condition in a nuanced, meaningful way."

By season nine, when over one hundred hours of *The Smurfs* cartoons had been created, the team had run out of comics to adapt and professions to pluck from the phone book—whereupon the writers and producers sent the Smurfs journeying through time to encounter versions of characters such as Gargamel, Hogatha, and

RIGHT | In this piece of artwork from Hanna-Barbera, Laconia the mute wood elf shows Smurfette the sign for butterfly.

Paul Winchell: Evil Wizard or Medical Hero? Both!

Paul Winchell (1922–2005) may have voiced the villainous Gargamel, but the actor was also a medical hero, having contributed to the design of the first artificial heart in collaboration with Dr. Henry Heimlich (of Heimlich Maneuver fame).

Before becoming known as a children's entertainer and ventriloquist thanks to numerous appearances on television shows throughout the 1950s and 1960s, and his own program *Winchell-Mahoney Time* (1965–1968), Winchell studied pre-med at Columbia University. A noted inventor, Winchell also held patents for dozens of other inventions, including a disposable razor, a plasma defroster, a flameless lighter, and battery-heated gloves. In the 1980s, he focused his attention on ending world hunger by developing a method of farming freshwater fish in sub-Saharan Africa.

Despite all of these accomplishments, Winchell is best known for entertaining generations of children as a voice actor whose distinctive roles included Tigger from *Winnie the Pooh*, Dick Dastardly from *The Perils of Penelope Pitstop*, and, of course, the Smurfs' chief menace!

Scruple specific to a certain historic place. To many, it marked the point when *The Smurfs* "jumped the shark"; regardless, it would be the *The Smurfs'* last season.

Hanna-Barbera would animate the characters only one other time, for *Cartoon All-Stars to the Rescue*, a prime-time special that ham-handedly delivered an antidrug message to kids via their favorite cartoon characters. As they were reluctant to combine a drug message with the Smurfs out of concern that very young audiences would not understand, Peyo and company limited the Smurfs' use to the opening sequence.

By 1990, *The Smurfs* had been cancelled by NBC, which by this point was getting rid of its animated Saturday morning lineup to allow for more news programming and the creation of a weekend edition of their hit *Today Show*. The "Golden Age of Saturday Morning" was indeed over, but there's no doubt the Smurfs had been key players in its existence.

Smurfs Alive!

The Smurfs animated series was responsible not only for popularizing the characters in America, but also for bringing them into millions of homes in over

OPPOSITE | Paul Winchell c. 1953 with dummies Jerry Mahoney and Knucklehead Smiff. **RIGHT |** Peyo and his studio were very involved in the creation and design of new characters for the animated series, such as Scruple, who first appeared in season six.

forty-seven countries including Italy, Spain, Mexico, Brazil, and Thailand.

In addition, the cartoons opened the door to numerous licensing opportunities that soon had the Smurfs appearing on thousands of products sold the world over, from bedsheets to breakfast cereals. In 1982 alone, Smurfs merchandise was estimated as bringing in $600 million in retail sales.

Equal efforts were made not just to bring the blue imps into households, but to bring families into the world of the Smurfs.

In 1984, Taft Entertainment, which at the time owned Hanna-Barbera, began to open Smurf-themed attractions at theme parks it ran through the Kings Entertainment Corporation. Smurf villages, water rides, and roller coasters became popular amusements at their Kings Island (Ohio), Kings Dominion (Virginia), Carowinds (North Carolina), and Great America (California) locations. The company even opened a Smurf Forest at Canada's Wonderland, near Toronto.

The Smurfs also toured stadiums as a part of the popular Ice Capades figure skating show. The costumes

LEFT | From top: A souvenir banner from the Ice Capades' "Smurfs Alive" presentation, and a variety of Smurfs memorabilia from 1959 to the present.

originally used in their 1982 *Smurfs Alive!* program were reused for other presentations, and distributed to their Ice Capades Chalets: stationary rinks located throughout America that offered regular entertainment and training programs for young skaters.

This kind of promotional blitz became the industry standard when dealing with children's entertainment properties during the 1980s. The practice drew the attention of organizations of concerned adults who argued that children couldn't tell the difference between an episode of *The Smurfs* and an ad featuring them. Yet they couldn't argue that it was the heart of the characters that drew the world's children, and legions of "grownups," to everything Smurfy. Since the characters went global, over two-thousand companies have been responsible for producing Smurfs memorabilia.

Stephen Parkes, a thirty-plus-year collector and holder of the 2011 Guinness World Record for most Smurfs owned, sums up the characters' cross-market, cross-generational allure: "I think it's their ideals, the fact that they are so helpful, have no vices, and appeal to a wide audience from kids right up to adults."

RIGHT | Peyo finds himself waist high in only a sampling of the Smurfs merchandise available in the early 1980s.

Bonsoir, Papa

On Christmas Eve 1992, Pierre "Peyo" Culliford died of a heart attack. The Smurfs had lost their true Papa. And although their television show—the medium through which millions had come to know them—had ended, the Smurfs continued to live on through the 1990s, thanks in large part to the efforts of the Culliford family.

International Merchandising, Promotion & Services (I.M.P.S), a company founded in 1984 by Peyo's daughter Véronique, continued to license the property throughout the world. While American companies were shutting down their Smurf theme park attractions, I.M.P.S. was arranging for Big Bang Schtroumpf to open in Lorraine, France. Even though the property changed hands a number of times since opening its doors in 1989, the park remained Smurf-themed until 2003.

The Smurfs also continued to appear in new comics produced by Peyo's studio and distributed by Le Lombard in Europe. Although his son Thierry had long ago assumed control of the studio (calling it Cartoon Creations) and other artists had been drawing the characters for years, Peyo's monograph remained on all new artwork that featured the Smurfs, Johan, or Benoît Brisefer—the mark of a proud papa.

LEFT | By 1982 Peyo had become the head of a global media empire. Toward the end of his life he returned to creating new comics, starting with the album *L'Aéroschtroumpf* in 1989.
OPPOSITE | The Smurfs' "Papa" at his desk in 1983.

And what had to happen, happened. Discord, enmity, jealousy--feelings till then unknown to the Smurfs-- destroyed the lovely harmony that had heretofore prevailed among them.

Oh! Hefty Smurf, Shmefty Smurf! He looks strong, but deep down, he's not as strong as all that!

I despise you!

Someone broke my guitar! And I was smurfing a serenade to Smurfette!

Ha! Ha! Well done!

And I hate you!

Hey, Brainy! You, go smurf me some...

Not now Papa Smurf! Later!

Me, I hate Smurfs who like Smurfette!

of the Smurf Village. Yvan Delporte introduced it to the comics because he found the name magical, and the word seemed so foreign to Peyo that he originally believed his partner made it up. An actual plant native to the Americas, sarsaparilla (*smilax regelii*) is commonly used on the other side of the Atlantic as the basis of soft drinks, namely root beer. As the plant was by no means exotic to Americans, references to sarsaparilla were changed to Smurfberries and Smurfberry bushes when the writers of the cartoon began adapting the comics.

ABOVE | Smurfs demonstrate various uses of the word "smurf" in a panel from *The Smurfette*. **RIGHT |** A Smurf happily chomps on a "sarsaparilla" leaf.

Smurfs of Note:
Now that we understand the basics, and can sound a lot smurfier at dinner parties, scientific symposia, and comic conventions alike, the following is a glossary of some of the key players from the comics and cartoon series that left their tiny footprints on the hearts and minds of countless fans.

Baby

Although the character known simply as Baby Smurf was dropped on account of a clerical error, the Smurfs are eventually allowed to keep him because of the love they show for the new arrival. In the animated series, Baby is depicted as magical and it is alluded to that he may be the next "Papa" Smurf.

Brainy

Called simply "le Schtroumpf à Lunettes" (the Smurf with Glasses) or previously called "le Schtroumpf Moralisateur" (Moralizing Smurf) in the comics, Brainy is one of the few Smurfs who has a history dating back to "Les Schtroumpfs noirs." In both the strip and the animated cartoon show, Brainy is depicted as a know-it-all who often gives condescending speeches to the others. While in the printed stories, he is punished for his haughty demeanor by a whack to the head with a mallet, the cartoon changed that to his being physically tossed out of the village—out of fear that viewers would hit children they didn't like on the head with a hammer.

Clumsy

Whether in the comics or the cartoon show, Clumsy is depicted as a good-hearted, well-meaning Smurf whose intentions are spoiled by his own two feet . . . which he falls over often. As he's somewhat dim-witted, it seems only natural that Clumsy's best friend would be Brainy, the self-professed smartest Smurf in the village.

named and modeled after the favorite childhood pet of Peyo's wife, Nine.

Puppy, a gift of Homnibus, arrived at the village bearing a locket only Baby could open, making Baby Puppy's true master. Yvan Delporte remembered the character as being the product of Hanna-Barbera's in-house formula to put a dog in all of their cartoons to broaden a show's appeal. However, when show writers created a blue Smurf-size pet for Baby, Studio Peyo objected and helped remodel Puppy into a magical creature in the shape of a "real" dog.

Scruple is Gargamel's young nephew and apprentice. He was introduced to the animated series in the 1986–1987 season, becoming one of *The Smurfs'* chief baddies. Like Hogatha before him, Scruple became more of a foil for Gargamel than the Smurfs. When he showed any interest in his uncle's hare-brained schemes, it was often to point out the obvious flaws or to poke holes in the wizard's theories.

Smoogle is Nanny Smurf's pink pet marsupial that she befriended during her time in Castle Captor. Like Nanny, Smoogle was rescued from the castle and goes on to live with the Smurfs in their village.

RIGHT | A colorful array of Smurf stickers.

21st SMURFERY

WHILE THEY MAINTAINED their profile in their native Europe, and especially in French-speaking countries where new comic albums were released regularly, for the most part, the Smurfs were viewed as a piece of '80s nostalgia. This was definitely the case in America, where the cultural landscape had begun to produce new fads and marketing booms before the old ones even had a chance to bust.

As the animated heyday of the Smurfs drifted further into memory with the passing decades, fans and critics wondered: Could tiny gnomes that traveled via storks and snail carriages find their way in the twenty-first-century world of internet super highways?

Absosmurfly.

Collectors' Market

While still active in Belgium and France, especially in the pages of Cartoon Creations' *Schtroumpf* magazine, which featured new Smurfs comics, American and British Smurf fans found the 1990s a little less smurfy. With no new cartoons and translations of the comics not readily available, the stream of Smurf merchandise, seemingly endless only a few short years before, had all but dried up on the shores of the United States and the United Kingdom in the 1990s.

This drove collectors to examine their preexisting wares a little more closely and share what they had with the world. The internet, still in its infancy, provided just the right avenue for a global community to

develop. Internet fan sites and online collectors' clubs began to populate the web.

"Until the internet I genuinely thought that I was the only person who collected Smurfs . . . well, certainly one of the very few who still collected them!" recalls Alan Mechem, a lifelong Smurf collector and host of the BBC's *Retrospectacular*, a program about pop culture collectibles. "Belgium certainly has the edge nowadays [in terms of new material being available]. It's amazing going there and seeing the Smurfs so popular . . . in every toy shop and even painted on walls."

As a result of the cultural exchange among collectors, people became aware of promotions that were happening across the globe and of holes they didn't realize were in their collections. "I think the most positive experience is meeting other Smurf collectors," says collector Stephen Parkes, who achieved his own place of note in the global Smurf Village in the pages of the *Guinness Book of World Records*. He admits that it was only through the help of the Internet community that he was able to achieve his record-holding collection of over 1,061 Smurfs and counting (the count was over 1,200 as of October 2010). "They are true to the nature of the

LEFT | (CLOCKWISE FROM TOP) A complete "mini-pixi" village (among the hardest-to-find collectibles), a Smurf Collectors Club card, and an assortment of European board games.
PREVIOUS | A diorama featuring PVC figurines made available by Schleich from the 1970s to the present.

Smurfs and are always really friendly and willing to help. Just like the Smurfs!"

However, both Mechem and Parkes are quick to point out that there are a few "Gargamels" out there on the internet, some of whom—like the villain himself—have tried to pass off their own creations as original Smurfs to improperly and illegally meet the demand for rare collectibles with bogus supply. To some, even collecting "fakes" has become a part of the hobby itself, and a market has sprung up around them, turning quite a profit for unscrupulous dealers and uninformed traders on internet auction sites.

Mechem warns: "Stay away from weirdos and people to whom collecting is just a 'who has more' game . . . and stick to your morals. It's only worth the price you pay!"

The Red (and Blue) Scare

When a property reaches the heights of success that the Smurfs hit in the 1980s, it's bound to have some detractors ready to tear it down and conspiracy theorists looking for evil messages that simply are not there.

While the *Smurfs* comics had no overarching social or political agenda, some stories, such as "Schtroumpf

RIGHT | Just a few of Schleich's "Super Smurf" figurines, which incorporated larger accessories into their design such as bed sets, automobiles, and sport paraphernalia.

He Who Smurfs Last . . .

During the 1990s and early 2000s, the first generation of international Smurf fans was coming into its own and started creating books, movies, and television shows, and the effect of *The Smurfs* was felt in the flexing of creative muscles. It is said that the true test of any intellectual property or cultural landmark is the ability to be referenced in non-related media and to not only be the subject of parody, but also withstand it. *The Smurfs* certainly did that.

While serious scholars such as Umberto Eco gave a winking nod to the Smurf language in *Kant and the Platypus: Essays on Language and Cognition* (collected in 1997 and published in English two years later), screenwriters such as Richard Linklater and Richard Kelly had their deeply philosophical characters offer their thoughts of the nature of the Smurfs in *Slacker* (1991) and *Donnie Darko* (2001), respectively. Thanks to an episode of *South Park*, the film *Avatar* (2009) is colloquially called "Dances with Smurfs" because of the strong resemblance to the Smurfs that the Na'vi people bear in both color and lifestyle—a comparison *Avatar* writer/director James Cameron has publicly acknowledged and had some fun

with. *The Simpsons* depicted Lisa watching the very Smurf-ish cartoon called "The Happy Little Elves" and Adult Swim's parody program *Robot Chicken* featured numerous unflattering spoofs of the program, some of which featured members of the original Hanna-Barbera voice cast.

Saturday Night Live, which for decades has reflected popular culture back at us through the lens of comedy, has lampooned *The Smurfs* a number of times, the most laugh-inducing skits being their depiction of Smurfette as the star of her own reality show; their false advertisement for an "epic" *Smurfs* mini-series event that starred the likes of Sean Connery (actually comedian Darrell Hammond) as Papa; and a histrionic interpretation of *The Smurfs* theme by Celine Dion (Ana Gasteyer).

All the while, the original animated series remained in the periphery of the pop culture radar, shown in near perpetual reruns on the Cartoon Network and then on Boomerang, its "nostalgia" spin-off channel in America, and a variety of other networks worldwide. This allowed legions of preexisting fans to get their proper Smurf fix and new viewers to be introduced to the village.

Raja Gosnell: A few words from *The Smurfs'* director

"The Smurfs are so intricately woven into people's childhoods; I was of course a bit reluctant to take on the great responsibility of making this film. However, in speaking to [producer] Jordan [Kerner], I realized we both agreed very much on what the tone and look of the movie should be. Knowing that I found a great ally in Jordan helped ease my initial trepidation . . . I know how much these little blue creatures mean to generations of kids and adults all over the world, and I wanted to give them a movie that they will enjoy for years to come. The midzone between honoring the source material and creating a compelling, feature-length movie is a challenging place to be. I like challenges, so hopefully we've created something that the longtime fans and new acquaintances will both enjoy.

"I think the idea of taking the Smurfs out of their enchanted forest and dropping them in the middle of a modern, urban jungle like present-day New York, offered us plenty of unique twists on the story of the Smurfs. Within that context, it was important to me to bring out the fun, adventurous element of the film—I wanted to show the Smurfs getting out of their comfort zone, let them run around NYC, and see what happens!"

they encounter strange locales including Times Square and Chinatown, and a toy store where they're mistaken for toys themselves. Aided in their quest to get home by expectant parents Patrick and Grace Winslow, the Smurfs manage to escape the clutches of Gargamel and of Odile Jouvenel, Patrick's boss, who has promised Gargamel riches and respect if he can provide a potion that can make aging people appear youthful again.

Along the way, Patrick and Grace learn about the power of magic, not only the kind that comes from potions and spells but the kind that comes from love and family, while the Smurfs pick up some life lessons of their own. At the heart of their story is Clumsy Smurf, who feels responsible for getting the Smurfs into their predicament through his own clumsy actions. However, as he helps lead and fight the Smurfs out of their problems, he learns that he is capable of so much more than just tripping over his own canoe-size feet. Ultimately, the lesson of the film is that whether or not someone's generally clumsy or brainy or grouchy, everyone is capable of proving that they're more than just one thing.

To helm the film Kerner sought out Raja Gosnell, who as the director of *Home Alone 3* (1997), *Never Been Kissed* (1999), *Big Momma's House* (2000), *Scooby-Doo* (2002) and its sequel, and *Beverly Hills Chihuahua* (2008) not only

OPPOSITE | A box full of Smurfs! **RIGHT |** (TOP) Actors Jayma Mays and Neil Patrick Harris as expectant parents Grace and Patrick Winslow. (BOTTOM) Clumsy gets animated while talking to the Winslows.

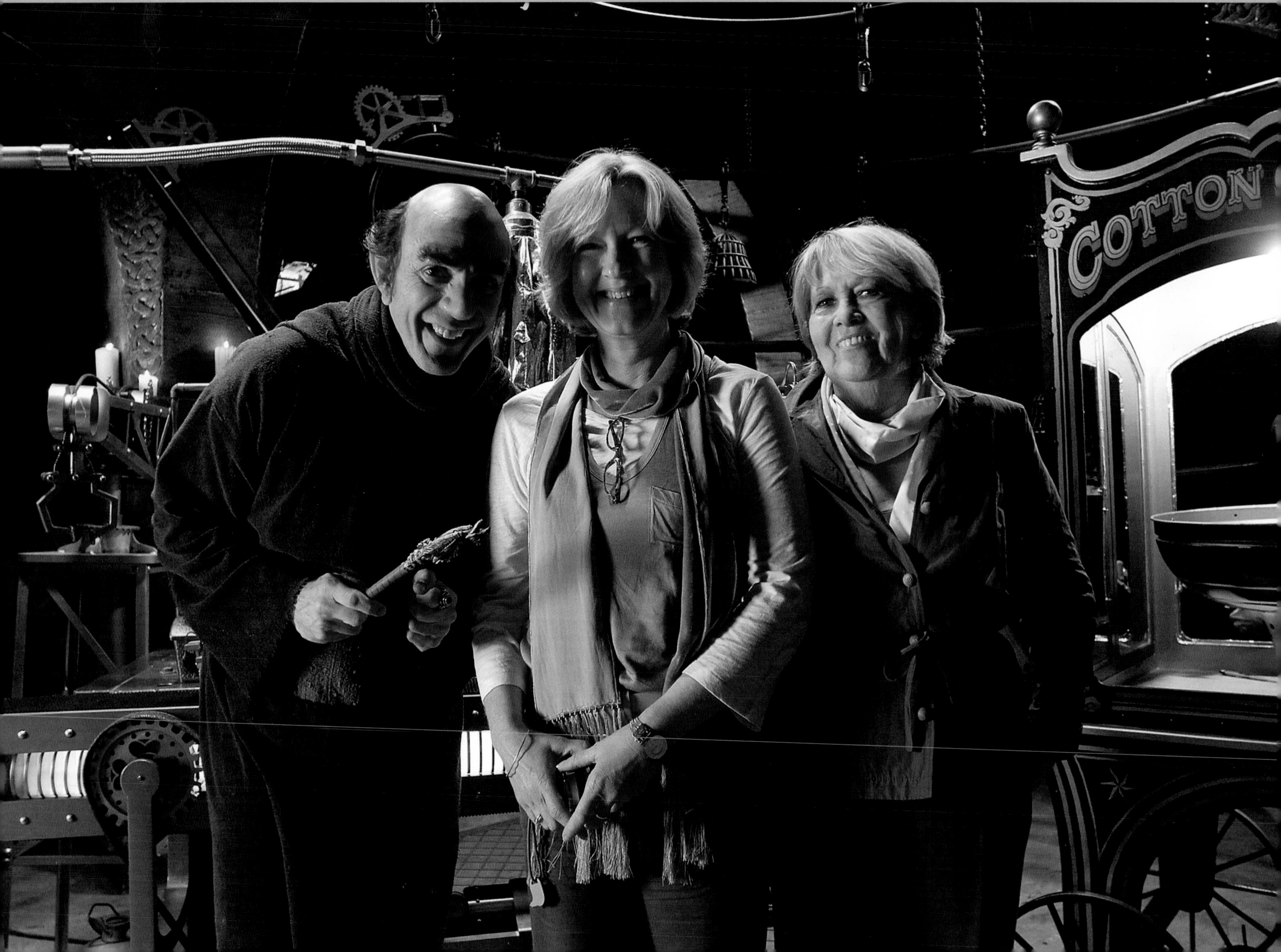
COTTON

Afterword

As a small child, Véronique Culliford was always a little frightened of Gargamel: "He was the bad guy, and so mean to the Smurfs . . . who isn't afraid of the villain?"

So, imagine her surprise when she and her mother, Nine, were invited to the set of *The Smurfs* by producer Jordan Kerner and brought to a dressing room where, "We met the real Gargamel and saw him in all his wicked and evil glory!"

Kerner recalls having to gingerly escort the president of I.M.P.S. across the room to where the Smurfs' tormentor cackled, spoke, and offered his crooked hand in greeting. "You could see Véronique's eyes well up," recalls Kerner of the meeting. "She told me it was from the joy of seeing Peyo's character in the flesh, but I think some of it was seeing her childhood nightmares come to life!"

Nightmare or not, for Véronique the experience truly was a dream come true.

"This [movie] was such an important milestone in the Smurfs' life that I'd brought my mum along with me as her eightieth birthday present," Culliford recalls. "She was obviously at my dad's side every step of the way on the Smurf adventure, much more so than I or my brother. In a way, the Smurfs were their children in an imaginary world. . . . We were given a very warm Hollywood welcome (even though we were in New York!) and that's always been a dream, but this time it was for real!"

And of Gargamel, who after some makeup removal—and reassurance that he wouldn't try to turn the Cullifords into gold or eat them—revealed himself to be actor Hank Azaria, Véronique has only the most stellar of reviews:

"'Gargy-Hank' really is fantastic . . . There's only one thing I can say: I absolutely love his interpretation of this character that I've always known and grew up with. His movements were exactly as they'd always been in my imagination, and yet he also added a certain human vulnerability to the character that I'd never imagined but that fits him perfectly."

Adding that new layer of discovery and enjoyment to the property on the whole was, of course, the reason to bring *The Smurfs* to a different medium in a refreshing way for a whole new era.

"We had to do something different from the comic and the cartoons," explains Véronique, "but also be there to make sure the Smurfs stay the same . . . [The filmmakers] believed in *The Smurfs*, which enabled us to believe in them while they made the film."

"Our overall goal," notes Kerner, "was to depict not only what was on the page, but what Peyo's intentions were when he created the characters. They transcend all of our views of characters like these . . . his creations are enduring."

OPPOSITE | "Gargy-Hank" with Véronique and Nine Culliford.